Table of Content

MW00593360

The Three Brothers and the Singing Toad, A Folktale .....

Folktale Follow-Up 15

Other Ways to Use *The Three Brothers and the Singing Toad* 16

Pocket Chart Activity 18

Story Mat 21

"The Elephant Counting Song" 24

Tissue Paper Banners 26

Lottery 27

Pottery Toys 30

A Spanish Conversation 32

Cooking Corn Tortillas 34

Weaving God's Eyes 35

Playing a Dancing Game 36

Celebrating Independence Day 37

How to Use the Counting Chart 39

Maya Weaving Designs 41

Paper Bag Piñata 43

Maya Mask 45

Mexican Flag 46

Map of Mexico 47

Glossary 48

Additional Resources ....Inside Back Cover

Our Philosophy

The world is a smaller place these days, and children in our classrooms are from many cultures. This series offers stepping stones toward the goal of mutual respect among children of different backgrounds. The program offers an integrated curriculum, with whole class, cooperative group, and individual activities for the primary grades. Interviews were the primary source of information for the program, giving the hands-on activities their authenticity, detail, and interest.

A special thank you to Margaret Azevedo, Griselda Morales
and Tekla White for their invaluable contributions to this book.

The Three Brothers and the Singing Toad

Retold by Betsy Franco

Spanish Words in the Story:

cenote (seh-noh´-teh) -- a deep natural limestone well
atole (ah-toh´-leh) -- drink made from corn
siesta (see-ehs´-tah) -- afternoon nap

There was an old farmer with three sons who took great pride in his large and well-kept cornfield. He was terribly unhappy one day when he realized that a large, mysterious animal was stealing his corn.

The farmer called his three sons to his side, "A thieving animal is destroying my corn. I will give my cornfield and everything I own to whichever of you can bring the animal back -- dead or alive."

     Mexico

The oldest son set out first. "All I need to complete this deed, father, is a good horse, a gun, and some atole. I will be back soon enough," he boasted.

When he had ridden nearly half the distance to the cornfield, he came to a deep cenote where he could rest and water his horse. Beside the cenote sat a small toad singing happily. The toad said,

> "I'm just a small brown singing toad,
> but listen carefully,
> To catch the tricky cornfield thief,
> you'll need a gift from me."

Mexico

The oldest son, feeling tired and hot, snapped back, "Why should I listen to a small toad?"

Then he picked up the brown toad, flung it into the deep cenote and continued on to the cornfield. Once there he sat through the hot afternoon and on into the dark and lonely night, until his eyelids were drooping with tiredness. But the thieving animal never appeared.

5   Mexico

When the oldest son returned home, he entered the house with his head down. His father, who could see that he had failed, said, "Since you have not completed the task, you cannot claim my cornfield and all that I own. Now it is your brother's turn."

The second son jumped up, ready to go. "All I need is a gun and some atole, and I should be back by dusk."

Mexico

When the second son reached the cenote, the toad was still there, singing his happy song. The toad said,

>"I'm just a small brown singing toad,
>but listen carefully,
>To catch the tricky cornfield thief,
>you'll need a gift from me."

"Keep quiet, simple toad, I'm trying to rest. I do not need the help of a toad, and I never will," said the second son.

At that, he picked up the toad by one leg and tossed it headfirst into the deep cenote. After a siesta to refresh himself, the second son hiked over to the cornfield. To his surprise, he spotted a large bird with beautiful white wings amidst the corn. As the bird took flight, the second son raised his gun and shot at it. Two large, milk-white tail feathers floated down from the sky, but the bird escaped. The second son collected the feathers and trudged home. On the way, he made a plan.

 Mexico

"I have found and killed the thieving animal," the second son boasted to his father and brothers. "I present you with its tail feathers."

But his father and two brothers were not fooled.

"You have only the feathers of the bird. You have not finished the task," said the father. "Now it is your brother's turn."

"All I need is a gun and some atole, please father," said the youngest son. "I will bring back the whole bird."

     Mexico

When the youngest son reached the cenote, the toad was singing his song cheerily. He said,

> "I'm just a small brown singing toad,
> but listen carefully,
> To catch the tricky cornfield thief,
> you'll need a gift from me."

The youngest son was pleased to see the toad and he replied, "Oh, thank you, small toad, for offering your help. Here, take some of my food. If you help me find the thief, I will keep you with me forever."

                   Mexico

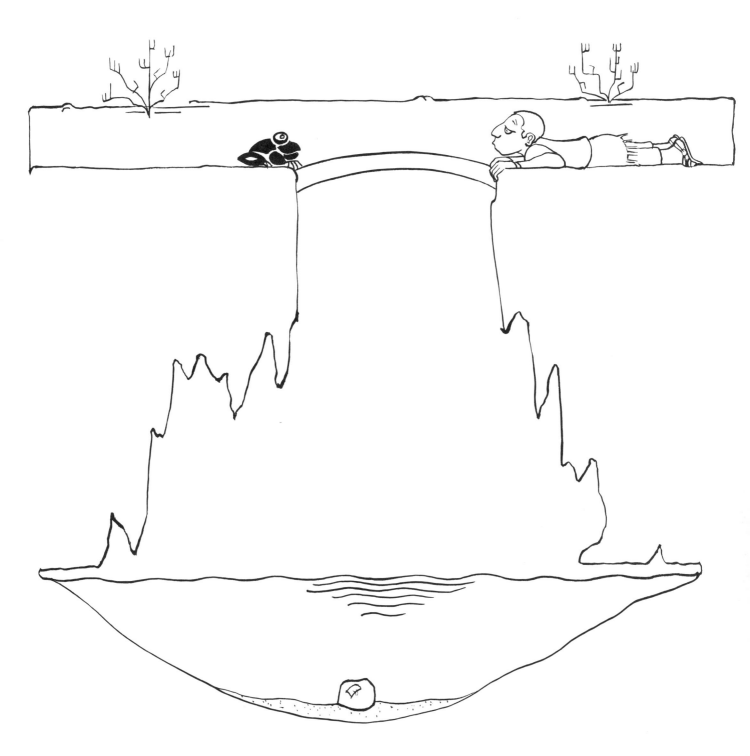

The toad was delighted.

"At the bottom of the cenote is a magic stone," he said. "It will grant you any wish."

"I would only wish for a kind and lovely wife and a way to catch the thieving animal that is stealing my father's corn," said the youngest son.

"Your wish will be granted this very day," said the small toad. "Not only that, but you will have a spacious home to live in with your new bride. Come with me now to the cornfield."

Mexico

As they approached the cornfield a large graceful bird appeared from behind a tree The youngest son took aim, but the toad jumped at his leg to stop him. Just then, the bird spoke, "Please do not shoot me. I am not really a bird, but a girl! An evil witch did this to me when I refused to marry her son. If you shoot me, you will be killing your own bride. You must believe me."

The youngest son was most surprised. But then he realized that his wish was coming true!

"Come with me, white bird, and I will take you home to my father and my brothers. With the toad's help and the promise of the magic stone, you will surely become a woman again, and you will be my bride."

   Mexico

The farmer and his other sons were shocked to see the youngest son entering the doorway of the house with a large white bird and a small brown toad.

"I have brought you the thieving animal you asked for, father. But it is really a woman who was cruelly bewitched. With the toad's help and the stone's promise, she will be changed before your eyes."

The toad sang his song heartily. The room became silent except for the toad's singing. Before their eyes, the white bird changed into a lovely young woman. Out the window, all could see a spacious home where none had been before.

"You have found the thief, my son, as well as a lovely bride. You shall receive my cornfield and all that I own in return," said the farmer.

The youngest son married the young woman, and they lived in the spacious home with the farmer, who was very happy in his old age. The two older brothers, who were jealous and disgusted, ran off and were never seen again. The small brown toad sat every day on the patio of the house and sang his cheerful song.

 Mexico

Folktale Follow-Up

Since this is a Maya Indian folktale, you might want to explain to the children that there were many groups of Indians in Mexico a long time ago. The Maya were one of the main groups. Some people in Mexico today are Indian or part Indian.

1. What do you notice about the way the characters are dressed?

The young woman in the tale is wearing a typical Maya dress. It is white embroidered cotton with a slip at the bottom. **Rebozo** (reh-boh´-soh) is the name for the long shawl worn by the women. The Maya brothers are wearing white pants and white shirts. Even today, some Indians still wear this type of clothing. In the cities, people usually wear modern clothes.

2. Share facts about the Maya house.

Maya homes had thick, white-washed adobe walls and straw roofs. Adobe is a mud brick. The thick walls kept the house cool. There was a doorway, but often no door. The beds were hammocks, slept in crossways. A fire in the center of the dirt floor killed the insects and sealed the roof.

Today, in the villages, some Indians still live in houses such as these. In the cities the homes are modern.

3. What can you say about Mexican food from the story?

Corn was considered the gift of life. It was thought that the serpent feathered god [**Kulkulkán** (Kool-kool-khan´) to the Maya and **Quetzalcoatl** (Keht-zehl-koh-ahtl´) to the Aztecs] gave the people corn.

In the story, the farmer had a large cornfield and the brothers took along atole, a drink made from corn. Corn is still a basic food in Mexico. Long ago and nowadays as well, tortillas are made from ground corn.

Mexico

Other Ways to use *The Three Brothers and the Singing Toad*

• Reproduce the story several times. Staple each copy inside a cover. Send the copies home with different children each night until all students have had an opportunity to share the story with their family. You may want parents to write a comment on the back cover explaining how their family shared the book and how they felt about it.

• If your students are at a level where they can read the story themselves, reproduce several copies for children to use for shared reading.

• Once your students are familiar with the story, reproduce the pictures on page 17. Have children cut the pictures apart and put them in the sequence they occur in the story. The pictures can then be used to...

1. Paste the story in order onto a large sheet of paper.

2. Create a picture book.
  • Paste the pictures into a book.
  • Use the pictures as you retell the story to a friend.

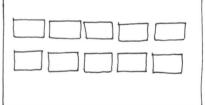

3. Rewrite the story.
  • Paste each picture to a sheet of writing paper.
  • Write about that part of the story.
  • Staple the finished pages together in order.
  • Make a cover for your book.

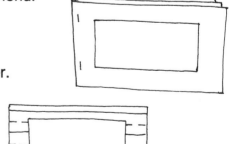

Mexico

Note: Reproduce this page to use in retelling the story of **The Three Brothers and the Singing Toad**.

Pocket Chart Activity

Cut out the strips on pages 19 - 20 and place them in a pocket chart.

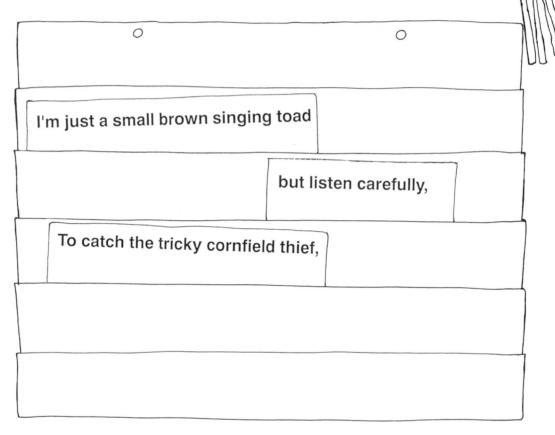

I'm just a small brown singing toad

but listen carefully,

To catch the tricky cornfield thief,

The chant can be read over and over again:

• It can be read after the first reading of the folktale and chanted again and again. Then in the second reading of the folktale, the children can join in on the verses.

• It can be read prior to the folktale.

Below are some suggestions for this particular chant:

• Talk about the contraction I'm. Have children find the other contraction in the chant (you'll).   Introduce other contractions, such as he's, she's, don't and can't.

• Cover up the word me and have the children fill it in using rhyming clues. Talk about the rhyming words, carefully and me, and ask the children to find other words that rhyme with me. They might even think of another verse for the toad to say.

        Example: I'm just a small brown singing toad,
                                but listen carefully,
                                Your brothers threw me in the well
                                and skinned my little knee.

I'm just a small brown singing toad

but listen carefully,

Mexico

To catch the tricky cornfield thief,

you'll need a gift from me.

Mexico

Story Mat

Paste to page 22

Mexico

Characters

Color in.
Cut out.
Fold.
Glue.

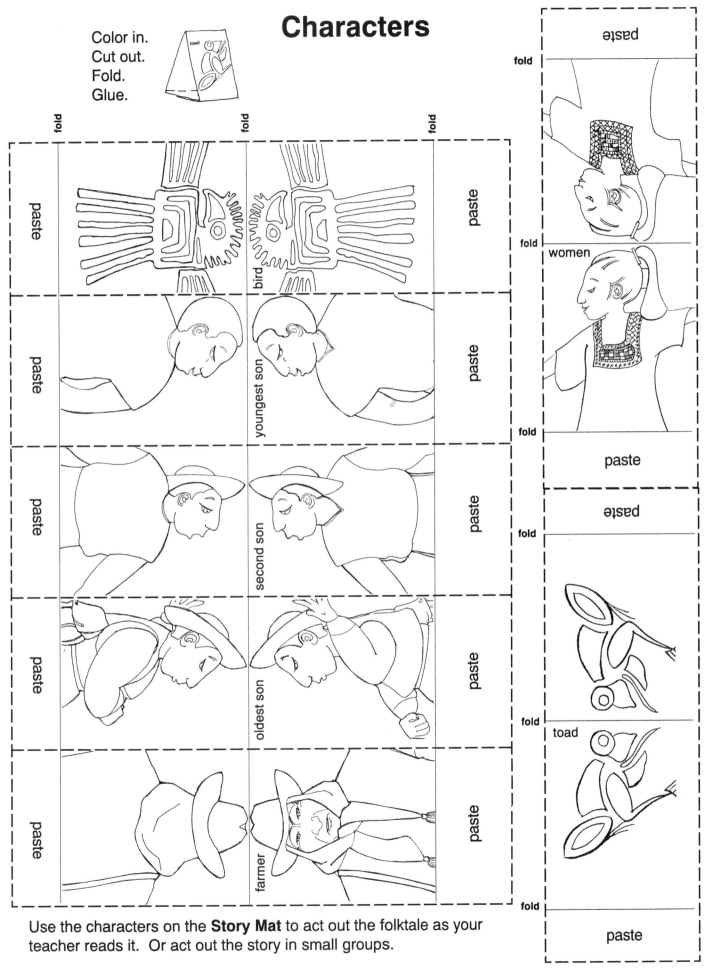

fold   **fold**   **fold**

paste   bird   paste

paste   youngest son   paste

paste   second son   paste

paste   oldest son   paste

paste   farmer   paste

paste

women

paste

paste

toad

paste

Use the characters on the **Story Mat** to act out the folktale as your
teacher reads it. Or act out the story in small groups.

    23   Mexico

Singing "The Elephant Counting Song"

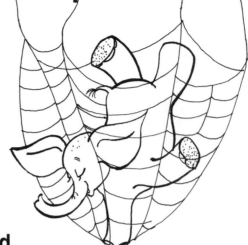

Cultural background

In Mexico, the primary grade children usually start the day by greeting their teacher and singing a song. "The Elephant Counting Song" translates as follows:

> One elephant was balancing on a spider web.
> Because it seemed so strong, he called another elephant.
>
> Two elephants were balancing on a spider web.
> Because it seemed so strong, they called another elephant.
> *(Repeat the verse until you reach ten.)*
> Ten elephants were balancing on a spider web.
> Because it seemed so strong, they called another elephant.
> BOP! *(The spider web breaks.)*

Counting in Spanish is as follows:

1	uno (oo´-noh)	6	seis (seh-ees)
2	dos (dohs)	7	siete (see-eh´-teh)
3	tres (trehs)	8	ocho (oh´-choh)
4	cuatro (kwah´-tro)	9	nueve (noo-eh´-veh)
5	cinco (seen´-koh)	10	diez (dee-ehs)

Preparation

You might want to familiarize yourself with the melody of the song and the Spanish words. Half of the song is in Spanish and half in English.

Mexico

Note: The more difficult Spanish words have been left in English for non-Spanish speaking children.

The Elephant Song

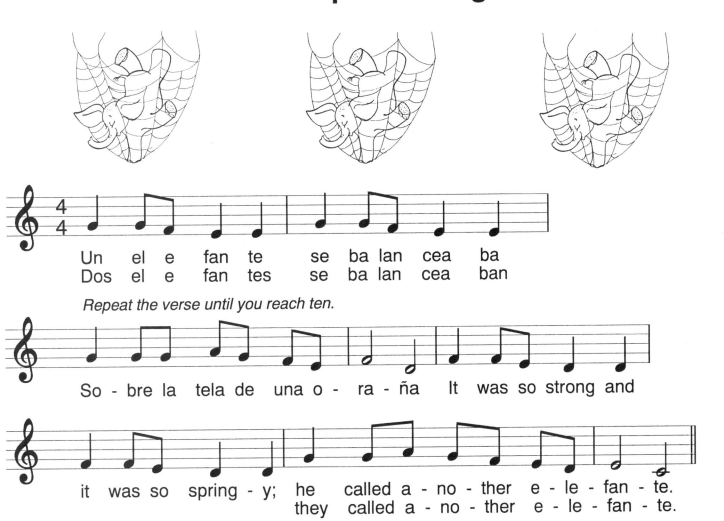

Un el e fan te se ba lan cea ba
Dos el e fan tes se ba lan cea ban

Repeat the verse until you reach ten.

So - bre la tela de una o - ra - ña It was so strong and

it was so spring - y; he called a - no - ther e - le - fan - te.
they called a - no - ther e - le - fan - te.

Pronunciation:

Oon eh-leh-fahn´-teh seh bah-lahn-seh-ah´-bah
Soh´-breh lah teh´-lah deh oo-n(ah) ah-rahn´-yah

Dohs e-leh-fahn´-tehs seh bah-lahn-seh ah´-ban
Soh´-breh lah teh´-lah deh oo-n(ah) ah-rahn´-yah

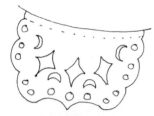

Tissue Paper Banners

Cultural Background

At fiestas, tissue paper banners with cut-outs are used to decorate homes and streets. Because of the texture of tissue paper, it is called "papel de seda" (pah-pehl´ deh seh´- dah), which means "silk paper." For use in the Independence Day celebration on page 37, you might want to have your children make their decorations in red, green, and white.

Preparation

For each pair:
• 2 rectangular sheets of tissue paper
• scissors
• hole punch
You will need string and a stapler.

Activity

• Pair up the children so they can help each other hold the paper during the cutting stage.
• Demonstrate the following steps. (You can demonstrate with waxed paper on the overhead projector or with a sheet of tissue paper.)

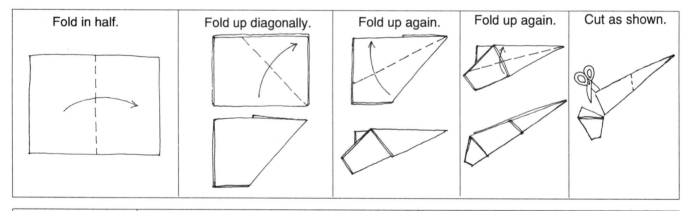

Fold in half.   Fold up diagonally.   Fold up again.   Fold up again.   Cut as shown.

Cut a design along the wide end like scallops. Punch holes.

Make decorative cuts along the bottom edge. Don't cut too near the top.

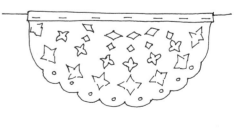

Fold the top over onto a string, staple and hang up!

 Mexico

Lottery
Playing a Board Game

Cultural Background

On Saturdays and holidays, adults in Mexico often play a game similar to lotto, called La Lotería (Lah Loh-teh-ree´-ah). The game cards have pictures of objects that are common to the Mexican culture. When the "caller" chooses an object, he doesn't just say the name, but first gives a hint or recites a poem about it. Players mark their cards with corn or beans. The goal is to get three in a row.

Preparation

To play the game, each child needs:

For each child:
• popcorn kernels or beans
• a copy of pages 28 and 29
• scissors
• tape

Activity

• <u>Preparing the caller cards</u> - ask small groups of children to think of a hint or a poem to go with one or two of the pictures on page 29. (Assign them the picture.) Let them dictate or write their results. (E.g. Mirror -- "I see myself in your glass." Flowers -- "You smell so nice, I'll sniff you twice.") Copy the hint for each picture onto a small piece of paper to be placed in a bowl for playing the game later.

• <u>Preparing the game card</u> - Divide the class into groups of six. Have each child cut out nine of the pictures on page 29 and tape them together in a different way from every other member of the group. This will be his/her game card.

• Play the game by choosing a hint/poem from the bowl and reading it aloud along with the object's name. Players place a popcorn kernel on the matching picture on the game card. The first child with three in a row wins.

 Mexico

La Lotería

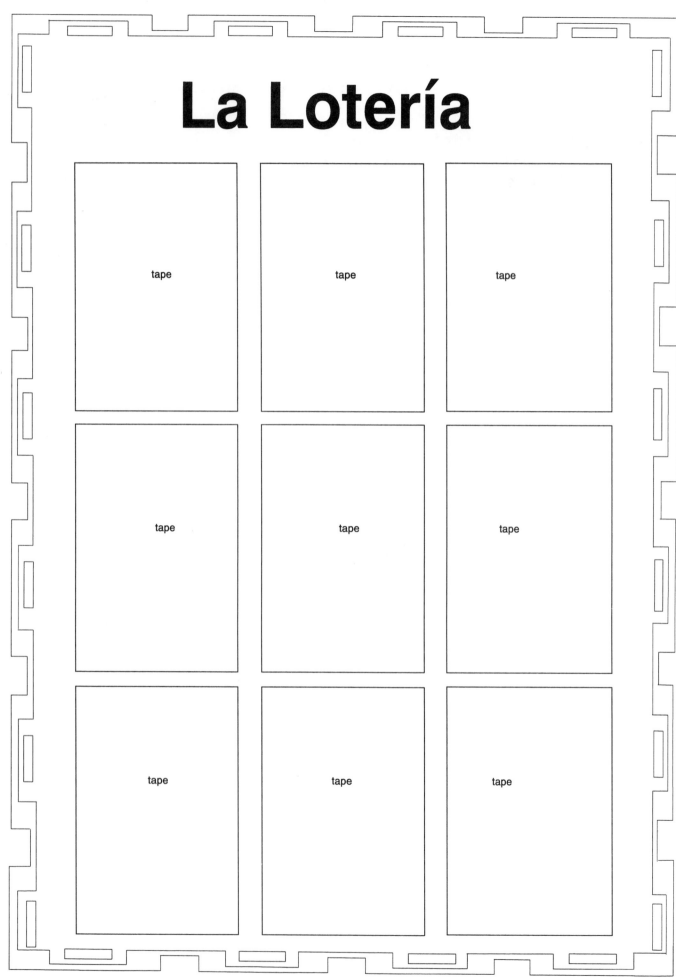

Mexico

Students use these pictures to play the Lottery game.

la estrella	la bota	la rana
la rosa	el pajaro	la corona
la compana	la mano	la pera
el nopal	el melon	el pescado
la araña	el tambor	la luna
el paraguas	el sol	la escalera

Pottery Toys

Cultural Background

Mexican toys include miniature replicas of items in the adult world, such as cookware, made out of terra cotta. There are also terra cotta animals, often with one hole in the back to use as a bank or two holes to use as a whistle. These pottery pieces come glazed or unglazed and are often painted in bright colors.

Preparation

For each pair of children: • modeling clay • a copy of page 31 • paint (optional)	You may want to make a sample pottery container about 1 to 2 inches high to show the children the approximate size of the toys.

Activity

• Divide the children into pairs.
• Hand out page 31. Explain the use of some of the cookware.

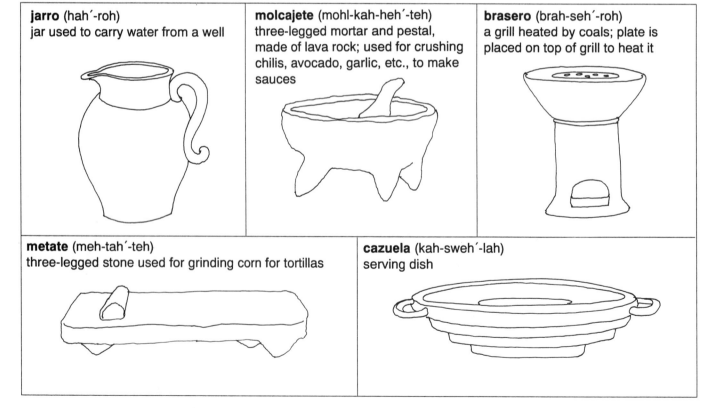

jarro (hah´-roh)
jar used to carry water from a well

molcajete (mohl-kah-heh´-teh)
three-legged mortar and pestal, made of lava rock; used for crushing chilis, avocado, garlic, etc., to make sauces

brasero (brah-seh´-roh)
a grill heated by coals; plate is placed on top of grill to heat it

metate (meh-tah´-teh)
three-legged stone used for grinding corn for tortillas

cazuela (kah-sweh´-lah)
serving dish

• Let the children make their own pottery toys out of clay.
• After the pieces dry, the pottery can be painted in bright colors.

 Mexico

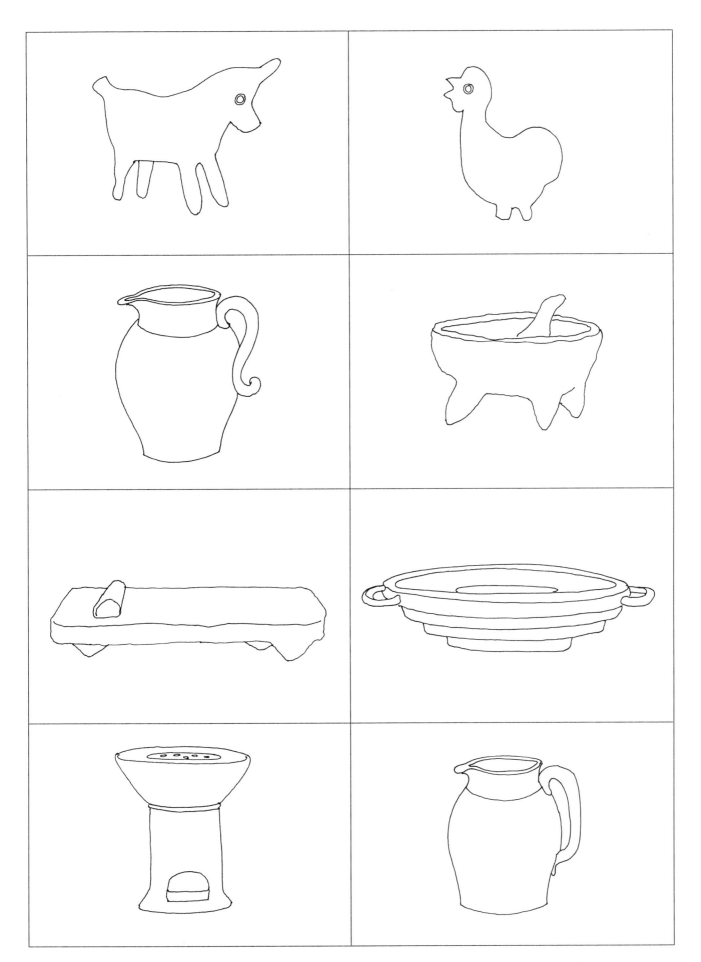

Mexico

A Spanish Conversation

Cultural Background

Spanish is a beautiful language that, unlike English, follows consistent rules for pronunciation. Mexican children learn English in school, so it would be nice for other children to know a few conversational phrases in Spanish. Notice that the question marks and exclamation marks are at the beginnings and endings of sentences.

Preparation

You might want to practice the conversation beforehand.

Activity

Practice each conversation separately. Take the part of person 1 sometimes, and let the children take the part of person 1 other times. Let the children practice in pairs once the phrases have become familiar.

	Spanish	Translation	Pronunciation
Person 1:	¿Cómo te llamas?	What is your name?	Coh-moh teh yah´-mas
Person 2:	Rosita. ¿Y tú?	(name of child) and you?	_____, ee, too
Person 1:	Fernando.	(Substitute name of child.)	
Persons 1 & 2:	Mucho gusto.	Nice to meet you.	Moo´-choh goo´-stoh

Person 1:	¡Hola! ¿Como estás?	Hello. How are you?	Oh´-lah koh´-moh ehs-tahs´
Person 2:	Muy bien. ¿Y tú?	Very well and you?	Mooee bee-ehn ee too
Person 1:	Bien, gracias.	Fine, thank you.	Bee-ehn, grah´-see-uhs
Persons 1 & 2:	¡Hasta luego!	See you later!	Ah´-stah loo-eh´-goh

Person 1:	¿Cuántos años tienes?	How old are you?	Kwan´-tohs ahn´-yohs tee-eh´-nehs
Person 2:	Siete años. ¿Y tú?	Seven years, and you?	See-eh´-teh ahn´-yohs ee too
Person 1:	Seis años.	Six years.	Seh-ees ahn´-yohs (Substitute actual age.)

                                       Mexico

Cooking Corn Tortillas

Cultural Background

One of the basic foods in Mexico is corn. Tortillas are made in several steps. Dry corn is soaked in lime (a chemical compound) and then cooked slightly. The corn is ground in a grinding mill and mashed on a stone. Next the ground corn is formed into thin patties, back and forth between the palms, and baked on a griddle or in a pan.

Preparation

For making 4 to 8 tortillas, each group will need:
- 1 cup (237 ml) corn flour (masa flour or Quaker harina)
- about 2/3 cup (158 ml) water
- mixing bowl
- duplicates of the instructions at the bottom of this page
  You will need a frying pan, cooking oil, and butter.

Activity

• Organize the children into groups of four. The instructions below can be duplicated for each group. You will cook on medium heat in a slightly greased pan.

Corn Tortillas

1. Put 1 cup of corn flour into bowl.

2. Add water a little at a time. Mix until you have a dry dough.

3. Form into balls.

4. Flatten balls to make patties.

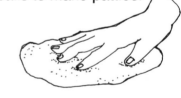

5. Cook in a little oil until you see brown spots on both sides.

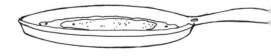

6. Butter. Roll up. Eat. Enjoy.

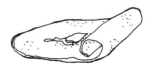

 Mexico

Weaving God's Eyes

Cultural Background

God's eyes or "ojo de dios (oh´-hoh deh dee-ohs) are traditionally woven on bamboo frames using colored yarn. They are often associated with protection. Fathers often start a weaving when a child is born and add onto it for each of the first five years of the child's life.

Preparation

> **Each child will need:**
>
> • colored yarn
> • sticks of different lengths
> (bamboo, shish kebob skewers, sticks from trees)

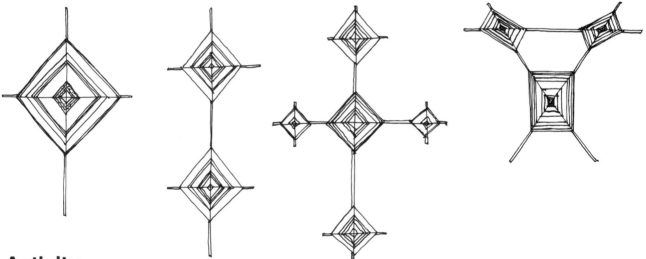

Activity

• Have the children decide on one of the arrangements shown above and take the sticks they need. (They can also make their own arrangements.)
• Start by tying the sticks together with one end of a piece of yarn. The knot should be in the back.
• Have the children get into the following rhythm: behind the stick and completely around the stick, behind the next stick and completely around, behind the next stick and completely around...
• Yarn of another color can be added by tying it onto the first piece of yarn.
• Talk about symmetry and help children decide if their creation is symmetrical.
• You can use a piece of paper to hide half the creation and then check if the other half is the same.

       Mexico

Playing a Dancing Game:
The Circle of San Miguel

Cultural Background

La Rueda de San Miguel (Roo-eh´-dah deh Sahn Mee-gehl´) means "the circle of San Miguel." This is a simple, fun dance that Mexican children do by skipping around in a circle. In the last line of the song, the child whose name is called out is the donkey. That child drops hands, turns outward, holds hands again, and dances around in that position. Eventually, everyone is facing outward. The translation is as follows (The words are somewhat nonsensical):

To the circle of San Miguel
All bring their box of honey, until it's ripe, until it's ripe.
May _____, the donkey, turn around.
Put child's name

Preparation

You may want to review the music and the words to the song.

Activity

• Skip in a circle, holding hands. Call out one child's name at a time to turn around.

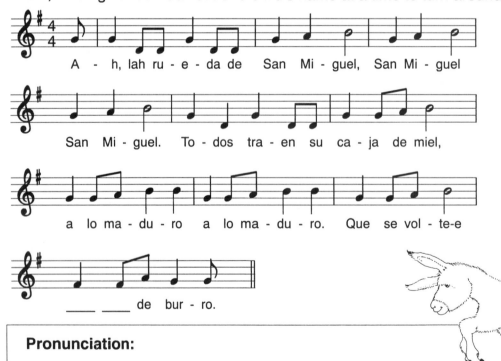

A   -   h, lah ru - e - da de   San   Mi - guel,   San Mi - guel

San   Mi - guel.   To - dos   tra - en   su   ca - ja   de miel,

a   lo ma - du - ro   a   lo ma - du - ro.   Que   se vol - te-e

____   ____   de   bur - ro.

Pronunciation:

Ah   lah   roo-eh´-dah   deh   Sahn Mee-gehl´.
Toh´-dohs   trah´-ehn   soo   cah´-hah   deh   mee-ehl´,
Ah   loh   mah-doo´-roh, ah   loh   mah-doo´-roh
keh   seh   vohl-teheh´_____   deh   boo´-roh.

36   Mexico

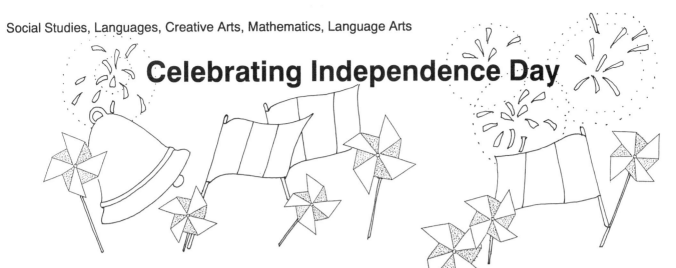

Celebrating Independence Day

Cultural Background

In 1810, Miguel Hidalgo y Costilla started the Mexican Revolution with a famous call (El Grito): ¡Viva La Independencia! ¡Viva Mexico! Independence Day festivities begin on the night of September 15. At 11:00 p.m., the President gives El Grito from a balcony. The people below repeat his words, a bell is rung, fireworks are set off, and flags and pinwheels are waved.

On September 16, there is a large parade. School children and adults march, charros (Mexican cowboys) ride on horses, and cars decorated with crepe paper flowers carry people dressed as the heroes of the Revolution.

The symbol on the Mexican flag came from the legend that the Aztecs built their civilization where they saw an eagle on a cactus eating a snake.

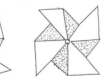

Activity

• Have the children work in pairs on the flags, flowers, and pinwheels.

• Decorate wagons and bicycles for the parade and hang the tissue paper banners made on page 26.

Choose a child to be President (perhaps a Spanish-speaker). Practice the events that will happen in the fiesta. Send home a note about wearing green, red or white on the day of the fiesta.

• On fiesta day, reenact El Grito with the President perched on a chair. Ring the bell and wave flags and pinwheels. Let the children parade with decorated wagons and bicycles. Some children can pretend to be charros.

• As a culminating activity, have the children write (or dictate) a description of part of the fiesta and illustrate it on a long mural. (Murals are an art form used by many famous Mexican artists.)

Flags

For the flag, each child needs:
- copy of page 46
- felt pens
- dowel, tape

Paint the flag red and green.

Use felt pens to color in the symbol in the middle of the flag.

Tape the flag to a dowel.

Crepe Paper Flowers

For the crepe paper flowers, each pair of children needs:
- 1 sheet of folded crepe paper cut in
5" - 13 cm lengths
- 2 twist ties

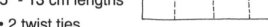

Fold the paper and cut the shape of a petal.

Spread out and overlap the petals.

Grab all the petals by their bottoms, in one hand.

Wrap the bottom of the petals with a twist tie.

Have your partner hold the bottom while you spread out the petals.

Pinwheels

For the pinwheel, each child needs:
- piece of square paper
- pencil
- tack

Fold and open.

Cut.

Fold every other tip inward.

Attach to a pencil eraser with a tack.

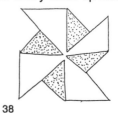

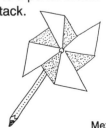

Mexico

How to Use the Counting Chart

Use the Counting Chart on page 40 to acquaint children with how they count to ten in Mexico. Leave the chart up in the classroom for the students to refer to while you are doing this unit on Mexico.

The chart also shows the symbols used by the ancient Maya. They had a number system based on 20 and used a symbol for zero. The numbers were written vertically.

rain

1	uno	6	seis
2	dos	7	siete
3	tres	8	ocho
4	cuatro	9	nueve
5	cinco	10	diez

wind

1. Provide students with many opportunities to count in Spanish. Let them count beans, maize, etc.

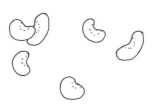

2. Students may enjoy creating a counting book about Mexico. Each page of the book could be a different number and the pictures could be of typically Mexican things.

3. Make a copy of the Counting Chart. Cut the numbers apart and let the students sequence the numerals as they count.

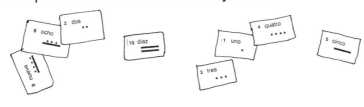

Counting Chart

1 uno ●	**6** seis ● ▬▬▬
2 dos ● ●	**7** siete ● ● ▬▬▬
3 tres ● ● ●	**8** ocho ● ● ● ▬▬▬
4 cuatro ● ● ● ●	**9** nueve ● ● ● ● ▬▬▬
5 cinco ▬▬▬	**10** diez ▬▬▬ ▬▬▬

Maya Weaving Designs

Cultural Background

The modern Maya maintain a connection with their past through myths, songs and legends which are handed down from generation to generation. The women weave designs representing the Maya symbols for the universe into their cloth.

Your students can create their own versions of these symbols, or create symbols for objects in their lives, using graph paper.

Preparation

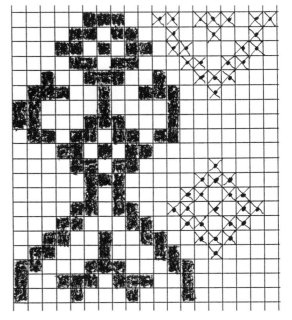

> **Children will need:**
>
> • form on page 42
>
> • crayons or marking pens
>
> • pencils

Activity

Show children examples of Maya designs. Explain that the designs represent something from nature and are woven into cloth that becomes clothing. Remind them that the design is a pattern which has to be repeated several times in a row. Encourage them to use bright colors as they complete their designs.

1. Think about how your design will look. How many times will you repeat the design?

2. Make light X 's with your pencil to show you which boxes to color.

3. Color in the design with bright colors.

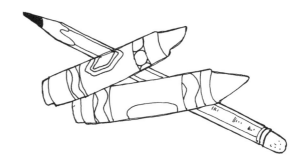

4. Write about your design.

 Mexico

Mexico

Paper Bag Piñata

Cultural Background

Piñatas are often used as part of the celebration of special occasions. They come in many shapes and sizes. The piñata contains special little treats such as candy and small toys. There is much laughing and joking as blindfolded children take turns trying to break the piñata with a stick. When the piñata is broken, everyone rushes to pick up the treats. The treats are shared among everyone present.

Preparation

You will need:
- large paper bag
- tissue paper in many colors
- construction paper in many colors
- copy of bird head pattern on page 44
- twine
- paste or glue
- scissors
- wrapped candy, peanuts, etc., to go in the piñata
- stick to hit piñata

Activity

Stuff the paper bag with newspaper before you decorate it. You will pull out the newspaper and replace it with wrapped treats before you staple the top and glue on the bird's head.

1. Cover the bag in tissue paper "ruffles."

2. Have children trace their hand on construction paper and cut it out. Paste the hands to the bag as shown to create the wings for the bird.

3. Add long narrow strips of tissue paper to form the tail.

4. Remove the newspaper and fill the bag with wrapped candy, peanuts, etc. Fold the top over and staple it. Glue on the bird head.

5. Attach the twine to the bag and hang it from a hook in the ceiling (or go outside and hang the bag from a tree or piece of playground equipment).

How To use:

Have the other children stand way back so there is no danger of anyone getting in the way of the swinging stick. Let each child have one swing at the piñata until someone manages to break it. Have children collect the treats. You may want to take the treats and divide them equally among your students.

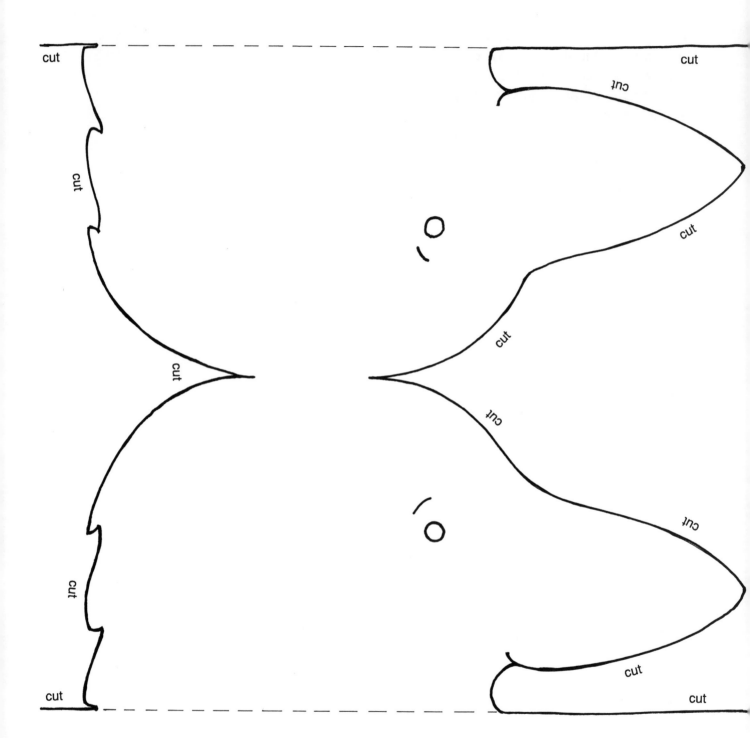

cut

cut

cut

cut

cut

cut

cut

cut

cut

cut

cut

cut

cut

cut

44

Mexico

Maya Mask

Color in.
Cut out.

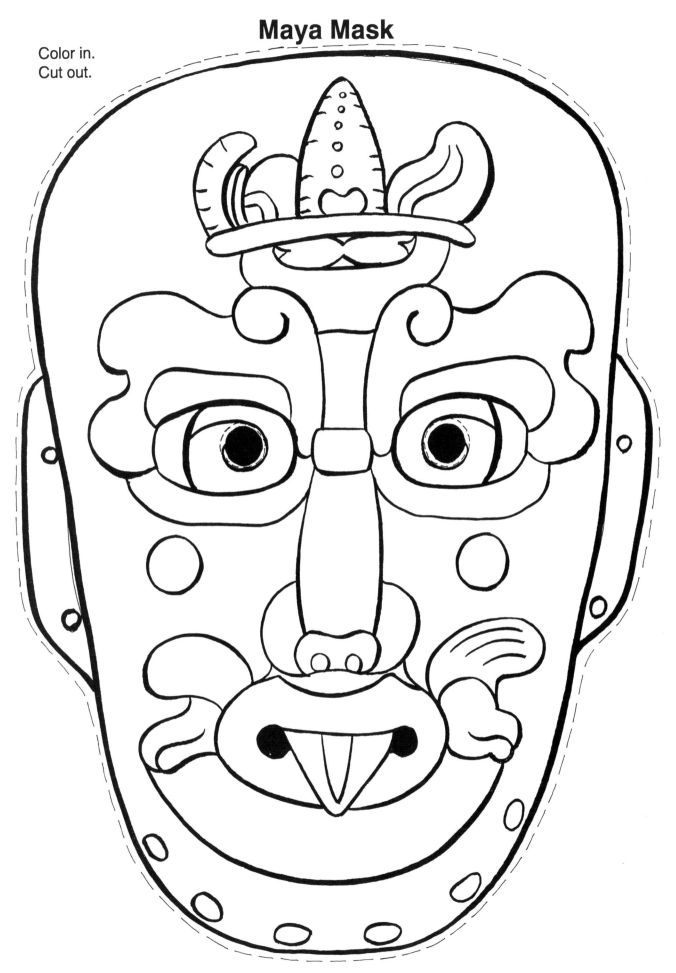

Mexico

Note: Use an encyclopedia to look up the colors of the Mexican flag.

Mexican Flag

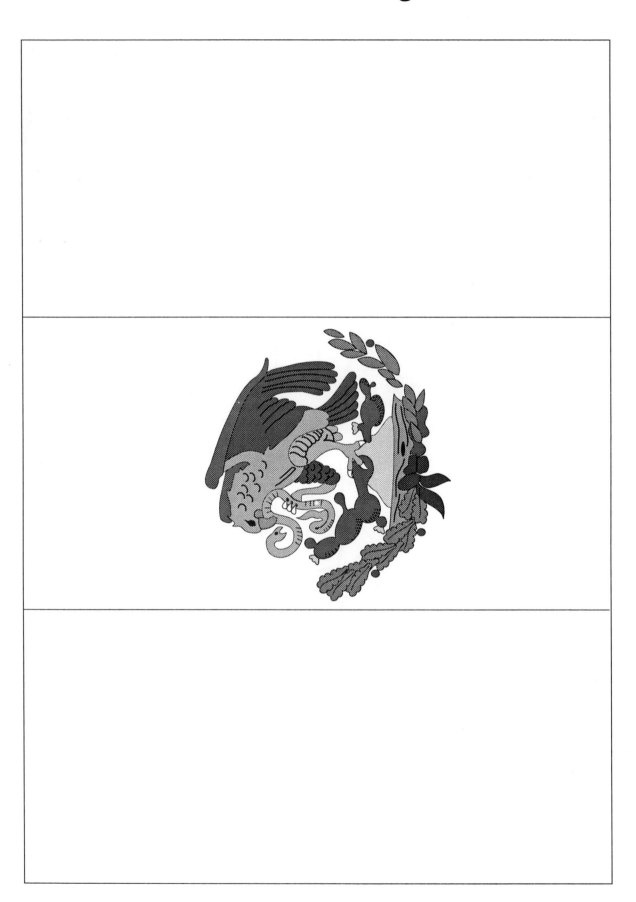

Mexico

Map of Mexico

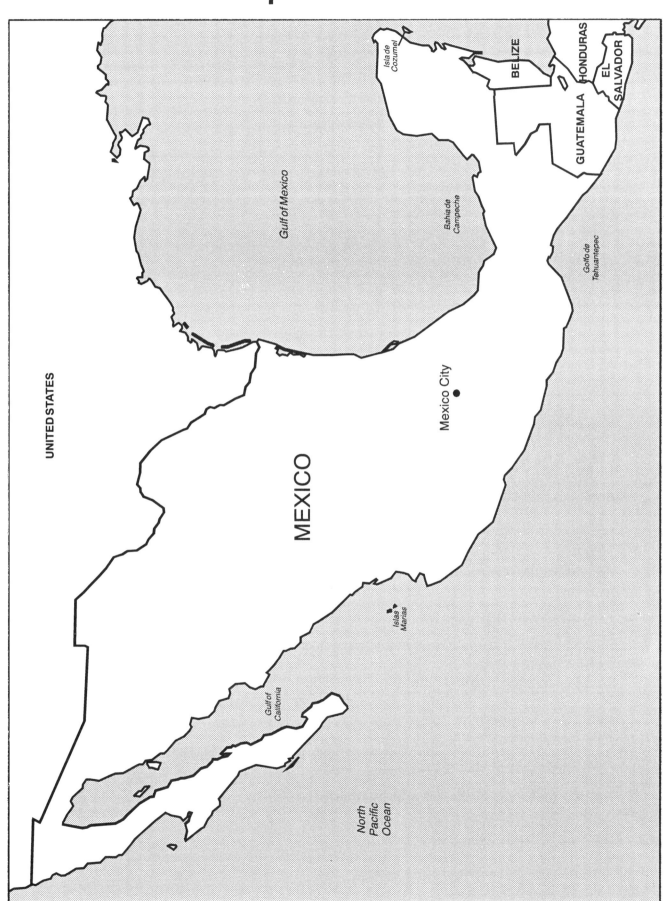

Isla de Cozumel

BELIZE

HONDURAS

GUATEMALA

EL SALVADOR

Gulf of Mexico

Bahía de Campeche

Golfo de Tehuantepec

UNITED STATES

Mexico City

MEXICO

Islas Marías

Gulf of California

North Pacific Ocean

Mexico

Glossary

adobe (ah-doh´-beh) -- mud brick

atole (ah-toh´-leh) -- drink made from corn

brasero (brah-seh´-roh) -- grill

cazuela (kah-sweh´-lah) -- serving dish

cenote (seh-noh´-teh) -- a natural limestone well that holds ground water

charros (chah´-rohs) -- Mexican cowboys

grito (gree´-toh) -- a call

jarro (hah´-roh) -- jar for carrying water

Kulkulkan (Kool-kool-kahn´) -- Maya name for feathered serpent god who is said

to have given the people corn

lotería (loh-teh-ree´-ah) -- lottery

masa flour (mah´-sah) --corn flour

metate (meh-tah´-teh) -- three-legged stone for grinding

molcajete (mohl-kah-heh´-teh) -- three-legged mortar and pestle

ojo de dios (oh´-hoh deh dee-ohs) -- woven god's eye

papel de seda (pah-pehl´ deh seh´-dah) -- tissue paper

Quetzalcoatl (Keht-zehl-koh-ahtl´) -- Aztec name for the feathered serpent god who

is said to have given the people corn

rebozo (reh-boh´-soh) -- a woven shawl worn by women; useful for carrying babies

rueda (roo-eh´-dah) -- circle or ferris wheel

viva (vee´-vah) -- long live